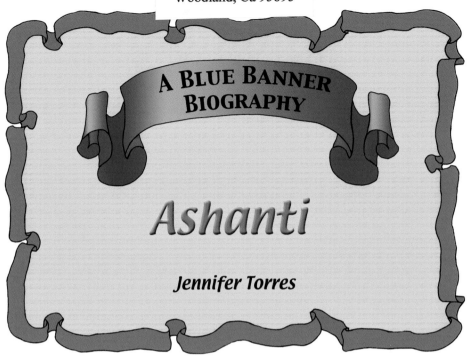

A BLUE BANNER
BIOGRAPHY

Ashanti

Jennifer Torres

Mitchell Lane
PUBLISHERS

P.O. Box 196
Hockessin, Delaware 19707
Visit us on the web: www.mitchelllane.com
Comments? email us: mitchelllane@mitchelllane.com

Printing   2   3   4   5   6   7   8   9

Blue Banner Biographies

Library of Congress Cataloging-in-Publication Data
Torres, Jennifer.
    Ashanti / by Jennifer Torres.
        p. cm. — (Blue banner biography)
      Includes bibliographical references (p.), discography (p.), and index.
      ISBN 1-58415-378-4 (library bound)
    1. Ashanti—Juvenile literature. 2. Singers—United States—Biography—Juvenile literature. I.Title. II. Series.
ML3930.A84T67 2005
782.42166′092—dc22

2004024410

ABOUT THE AUTHOR: Jennifer Torres is a freelance writer and newspaper columnist based in Central Florida. Her articles have appeared in newspapers, parenting journals, and women's magazines across the country and Canada. When she's not writing she enjoys spending time at the beach with her husband John and their five children, Timothy, Emily, Isabelle, Daniel, and Jacqueline.

PHOTO CREDITS: Cover, pp. 4, 11 Globe Photos; pp. 21, 23, 27 Wire Image; p. 28 Getty Images

ACKNOWLEDGMENTS: The following story has been thoroughly researched, and to the best of our knowledge, represents a true story. While every possible effort has been made to ensure accuracy, the publisher will not assume liability for damages caused by inaccuracies in the data, and makes no warranty on the accuracy of the information contained herein. This story has not been authorized nor endorsed by Ashanti.

CONTENTS

Ashanti loves to sparkle. When she attends special events she makes sure to always look her best.

Radio Days

"Turn down the radio!" commanded a voice from upstairs.

But 12-year-old Ashanti Douglas was busy, running a noisy vacuum cleaner across the carpet of her living room floor. She didn't hear a thing.

"Don't listen to the radio," said the voice again. "You'll take too long cleaning."

This time Ashanti heard the demand. It was her mother, Tina Douglas.

"Ma, that was just me singing," Ashanti said. "I wasn't listening to the radio."

She heard footsteps coming down the staircase. "That was you?" her mother asked.

Ashanti nodded her head yes.

"Let me hear that again!" her mother said in amazement.

So Ashanti began to sing her favorite song, *Reminisce*, by Mary J. Blige. As her mother listened, she realized that her daughter had a wonderful voice.

> **Now Tina realized Ashanti was a very gifted singer. Too good, her mom thought, to ignore.**

Ever since Ashanti was very small, Tina Douglas knew that her daughter had talent. But it was Ashanti's talent as a dancer that Tina — a dance instructor herself — had encouraged. Ashanti had been taking dance classes since the age of three and had become very good. So good, in fact, that she had performed at famous places like Carnegie Hall and The Apollo by the time she was ten. She also danced in the Disney TV musical *Polly,* which was directed by Debbie Allen and starred Phylicia Rashad.

But this was something new. Now Tina realized Ashanti was a very gifted singer. Too good, her mom thought, to ignore. So Tina got out a tape recorder and began to record Ashanti.

Many of the songs she sang were by Mary J. Blige, Ashanti's inspiration and favorite singer.

Soon Ashanti's mother began sending the tapes to record companies. Many singers looking to get noticed will make what is called a "demo." This is done in a studio with really good music and expert help. Not surprisingly, making a demo costs a lot of money.

Ashanti's house was always filled with music because her parents were also talented performers.

"We didn't have the money to go into the studio and record a demo, so when we went to meet with labels I had to sing and dance in front of all these people," Ashanti told Mark Daniels of Amazon.co.uk.

Performing for a crowd was something Ashanti was very comfortable with. Ashanti's house was always filled with music because her parents were also talented performers. Her mother was a dancer and her father, Kincaid Douglas, was a singer. Ashanti was very close to her family, which also included a younger sister, Kenashia. They lived in the town of Glen Cove, New York. It was a place with a lot of green trees, blue lakes, and friendly people.

When Ashanti was born on Oct. 13, 1980, her parents wanted to raise her to be strong and confident. Her mother named her after the Ashanti tribe in Ghana, a country in Africa. In this tribe the women are in charge. They are one of the most important tribes in Ghana and have a reputation for strength and determination.

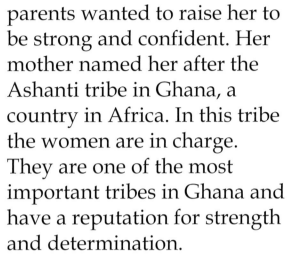

Her mother named her after the Ashanti tribe in Ghana, a country in Africa. In this tribe women are in charge.

Her grandfather, James Davis, also taught Ashanti a lot about being strong. He was a man who believed in the rights of all people. He had even marched with the famous civil rights leader Martin Luther King Jr. in the 1960s. He taught Ashanti that when someone tells you that you can't do something, you should try twice as hard to do it.

Ashanti went to church each Sunday. She never spent too much time away from home. She loved spending time with her family, watching cartoons, and playing with puppies. But after her mom made the demo tape, life started to move a little faster. Record labels were listening to the tape. One day, not long after Ashanti had turned 14, a call came from a record company. They wanted Ashanti to audition for them.

But this was no ordinary audition.

Sean "Puffy" Combs (who would become even better known when he changed his name to P. Diddy in 2001) would be there in person to hear her sing.

> *Sean "Puffy" Combs (who changed his name to P. Diddy) would be there in person to hear her sing.*

Paying Her Dues

*N*ot surprisingly, Ashanti was nervous when she arrived for the audition. As she belted out one of her favorite Mary J. Blige songs, she could tell that Puffy was impressed.

When Ashanti finished the song, she expected to see a recording contract in front of her. But instead, Puffy pulled out a bottle of cologne. He told Ashanti it was a brand-new scent and he really loved it. Then he asked Ashanti to smell it and tell him what she thought. Even though Ashanti was puzzled by the request, she leaned forward and took a little whiff of the stuff.

"One sniff and I'm like, "Oh pew, it stinks. I hate it," Ashanti told Mark Daniels. "He just started laughing. He said it was just a test to see if

I was a real person. I'm like, 'Well you know I am because that stinks.'"

Despite her honesty, Puffy didn't offer her a contract. It was a let down. Before she had time to be sad about it, she heard from Jive Records,

From the time she was a little girl, Ashanti loved to sing and her mother often found her singing and dancing around the house.

another record company. They wanted to see her right away!

Ashanti was very excited. She was also nervous. After all, her meeting with Puffy Combs had seemed to go so well but he didn't sign her. Ashanti was afraid the same thing would happen at Jive.

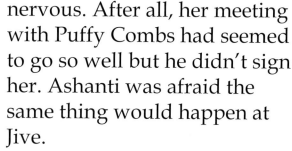

Ashanti sang her heart out at the audition and Jive signed her on as a new artist. She was thrilled!

Ashanti sang her heart out at the audition and Jive signed her on as a new artist. She was thrilled! Since Ashanti loved to write poetry, she decided she would also write her own songs. The first song she wrote was called *Can't Stop.* It was about a boy she really liked. Sadly, the song never got recorded. Ashanti soon realized Jive Records wasn't where she wanted to be. Known for handling the careers of top-40 pop artists like Britney Spears, the Backstreet Boys, and 'N sync, Jive just wasn't making the kind of music Ashanti wanted to sing.

"They were moving on to a pop path and I really didn't want to do it. I wasn't allowed to be too hands on, and I wasn't crazy about the music and the lyrics. I mean, I was young, but I'd been writing for a long time and I just didn't like the vibe," Ashanti explained to Daniels. "I didn't want to play the songs for my friends, so why would anyone want to play them on the radio?"

It was a hard decision. But she finally left Jive. "Jive just wanted her to be bubblegum music," said Brice Vick, a close friend of Ashanti, on the VH1 program *Driven: Ashanti.* "You know, Ashanti had her own style."

Ashanti went back to her life at Glen Cove High School. She joined the track team, the drama club, and the cheerleading squad. But she never gave up singing. She entered talent shows and kept singing in the church choir. However, school was important to her. She had a lot of friends. She got really good grades and she did very well in sports.

> *It was a hard decision. But she finally left Jive. "Jive just wanted her to be bubblegum music," said Brice Vick.*

"Not only was she a cheerleader but she was in the chorus and theater group so she had a chance to sing," said Cheryl Goodine, Ashanti's aunt and the assistant principal at Glen Cove High, in an interview with *American Cheerleader* magazine. "She also sang at her graduation. But it was when she sang the *Star-Spangled Banner* as a cheerleader at one of our pep rallies that everybody at school realized what a powerful voice she had."

Her friends at school remember Ashanti as an all-around good student and a good friend. One of them was Melissa Castro, who was also a cheerleader.

"Ashanti was a typical high school kid," Castro told *American Cheerleader*. "But she was known for having a beautiful voice and being an outstanding athlete."

Ashanti's athletic talent was about to force her to make a very important decision.

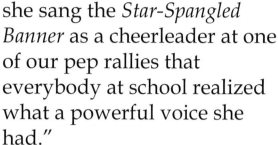

In high school Ashanti was known for having a beautiful voice and being an outstanding athlete.

A Tough Decision

*A*shanti was an exceptional sprinter who won many of the races she entered. She proved to be even better in the triple jump. She would run at full speed down the runway and push herself into the air. She would land on the same foot she used for her takeoff, push off again, come down on the other foot and launch herself for the third time before coming down into the sand pit. Her best mark was a distance of 33 feet, 9 inches. It was a school record.

As Ashanti got closer to graduation she received great news. She had won a track and field scholarship to attend Princeton University, one of the country's most prestigious institutions. Many students work very hard to get into Princeton, but very few are accepted. Ashanti was being invited to attend, and they would pay the bill!

But at the same time Ashanti found out about her scholarship, she received another offer. Epic

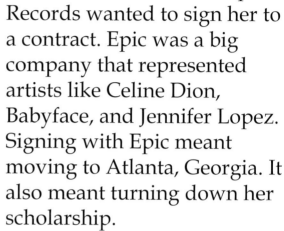

Now three schools wanted her very badly. But she couldn't pass up a chance at her dream.

Records wanted to sign her to a contract. Epic was a big company that represented artists like Celine Dion, Babyface, and Jennifer Lopez. Signing with Epic meant moving to Atlanta, Georgia. It also meant turning down her scholarship.

What was she going to do?

Then the decision got even harder. Ashanti was given the chance to go to two other good schools named Clark and Hampton. They also wanted her to be on their track and field teams. Now three schools wanted her very badly. But she couldn't pass up a chance at her dream. This was something she had always wanted.

So at the age of 17, she signed the contract with Epic Records.

Ashanti moved from her home in New York to Atlanta. She had to say goodbye to her friends, her family, and her room. It was scary but also exciting.

She lived in an apartment all by herself. At first she was happy to have a place all to herself. She could stay up late; have friends over anytime she wanted to; eat what she wanted; and there was no one to tell her what to do. But after a day at the studio, she was too tired to stay up late. She didn't really have any friends and she missed her mom's voice telling her to what to do. So when she wasn't in the studio, she spent a lot of time watching TV.

The days went by slowly. At first Epic seemed very interested in her career. But as time passed they seemed less and less interested.

At first Epic seemed very interested in her career. But as time passed they seemed less and less interested.

"When I was signed to Epic, I moved to Atlanta where they're based, to concentrate on the album," she told Mark Daniels. "I was 17 years old, living by myself in a different state. I had nobody there and nothing was going right. All my friends were going to college and having a ball and I was just sitting at home watching cartoons all day."

Friends would call and tell her about the colleges they were attending. She began to wonder if she had made the wrong decision. She had been accepted to three colleges. Now she was alone in Atlanta with no record to show for it.

Then something that was even more upsetting happened.

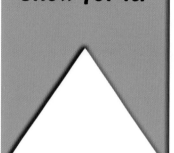

She began to wonder if she made the wrong decision. Now she was alone in Atlanta with no record to show for it.

"The guy who signed me left. When that happens you get shifted to the bottom of the list of priorities," Ashanti explained to Daniels.

Soon Epic had recorded enough of Ashanti's songs to put together an album. She started to hear her name on the radio, but the album's release date kept getting pushed back.

"It was hard for her when all her friends were away at school, and they would ask, 'So when is your record coming out?'" Ashanti's mother told Hyun Kim of *Vibe Magazine Online.*

Secretly, Ashanti began wonder if the record was ever going to be out.

A Light in the Tunnel

*L*ife alone at the age of 17 wasn't easy.

"It was very hard living in Atlanta because I was living on my own," Ashanti told Allissa Hosten of *Jet* magazine. "I was paying my own bills, my own car, everything."

Ashanti soon decided enough was enough. Her friends were having fun in college. Ashanti didn't know what to say to them when they asked about her record. Epic didn't seem to know when it would come out. They said the songs still needed work. Ashanti began to feel like they had stopped caring about the record. So she made a big decision. She left Epic and she left Atlanta. Her album was never released. Ashanti returned home. Two record deals had fallen through.

What was she going to do with her life now? She got a job watching kids in a daycare center. Just maybe, she thought, she wasn't meant to be a star.

Ashanti's mom became her manager. But instead of calling her a manager, Ashanti called her a "Momager."

She could follow the path her friends had taken and go to college, or she could keep trying to make it as a singer. Ashanti loved school, especially science. She thought being a medical examiner would be exciting. As a medical examiner she could study a person's body after they died to determine the cause of death. It was very different from singing to a crowd of people. But singing stardom just wasn't happening.

Ashanti's mother knew her daughter was ready to give up. Tina Douglas knew that would be a mistake. She thought there was no reason why her daughter should have so much talent and not be able to use it. So she took some control. From that point on Ashanti's mom became her manager. But instead of calling her a manager, Ashanti called her a "Momager."

The "Momager" started making some calls.

One call led to a break. It was to a friend who referred Tina to a woman who had once babysat for a little boy named Irv Gotti. Gotti was now a big name in the record industry.

Gotti introduced Ashanti to JoJo "Bangs" Brim, who worked for a label called Def Soul. Brim used Ashanti as a background singer on some songs. Then Chris Lorenzo, Irv's brother, called her to

Irv Gotti gave Ashanti her first real job in the music business. Ashanti sang on the song "How We Roll," which became a hit.

sing a part on a song called *How We Roll*. The song was written by a rapper named Big Pun who had died at an early age from health problems. Ashanti changed the words to the song a little and it became a hit.

But the public didn't know Ashanti yet. The video for the song was animated so nobody got to see her face. Behind the scenes, though, some big names began to know her name. Ashanti's talent as a song writer was getting noticed. She even wrote some lyrics for Jennifer Lopez.

"She listens and takes directions well," Brim explained to Hyun Kim of *Vibe*. "But she puts her twist on things."

In 2001 a song by Ashanti called *When a Man Does Wrong* appeared on the soundtrack to the 2001 movie *The Fast and the Furious*. But her big break came when Gotti asked her to sing backup on a song with a popular rapper named Ja Rule. The song was *Always on Time*. The music video made for the song showed the world who Ashanti was.

Her big break came when Gotti asked her to sing backup on a song with a popular rapper named Ja Rule.

Always on Time went to number one on *Billboard's* Hot 100 chart in 2002. At the same time, another duet Ashanti did with a rapper named Fat

When Ashanti's duet with Ja Rule called "Always on Time" hit number one on Billboard's Hot 100 chart, she knew she had really made it big.

Joe, called *What's Luv*, was heading up the charts too.

Both songs were being played on the radio a lot. Ashanti's friends were very excited for her. People started recognizing her name and her music.

It was the perfect time for Ashanti to release her very own album.

Both songs were being played on the radio a lot. People started recognizing her name and her music.

The Sky's the Limit

*O*n April 9, 2002, Ashanti's first solo album hit the stores. It was called simply *Ashanti*. On the very first day it sold 150,000 copies. By the end of the first week more than 500,000 copies had been sold. Ashanti wrote all 12 songs on the album.

The first song played on the radio was called *Foolish*. It jumped up the Hot 100 chart and landed in the top ten along with *Always on Time* and *What's Luv?* That gave Ashanti three top ten songs in the same week. She was the first female to ever accomplish that feat. The only other singers who have done the same thing are the legendary Beatles.

The album was a big success. Soon it hit number one on the album chart. It also went on to win a Grammy Award for the Best Contemporary R&B Album and eight *Billboard* Awards.

During this exciting time, Ashanti fulfilled another dream. She wrote a book of poetry. It was called *Foolish/Unfoolish: Reflections on Love.*

Ashanti was named the Aretha Franklin 2002 Entertainer of the Year during the Soul Train Awards.

"I've always enjoyed writing," Ashanti told writer Jeff Lorez. "It was fairly easy for me to write papers, essays, things like that. I used to win awards for it. I was actually in all honors English classes. I want to write children's books in the future, but for right now, the songwriting keeps me busy."

She also guest starred on the TV shows *Buffy the Vampire Slayer* and *American Dreams.* And Ashanti was very happy to be named as the Aretha Franklin 2002 Entertainer of the Year during the Soul Train Awards.

It was a thrilling time. But then something very sad happened.

"After eight years of waiting, Ashanti finally got her career started, and she finally got everything rolling, and everything began to open up and happen to her," said Ashanti's cousin, Meisha Douglas on *Driven: Ashanti*. "And then her grandfather died."

Ashanti heard the tragic news just before a show. She loved her grandfather, James Davis, so much. Now she wasn't sure she could sing in front her fans. Then she thought of the lessons he had

Not only was her music climbing up the charts but Ashanti also earned four American Music Awards in 2003.

taught her. He taught her to be strong. Her fans were filled with love for her. Ashanti knew she could do the show. She was strong, just like her grandfather had taught her to be.

On July 1, 2003, Ashanti released her second album, *Chapter II*. It also went to number one on the *Billboard* 200 list. One of her favorite parts of

Ashanti calls her mom Tina Douglas, her "momager," because she is part mom, part manager.

the album is a song she did with her sister Kenashia.

In 2004 Ashanti's third album *Concrete Rose* debuted and hit the *Billboard* 200 chart again in the top 30.

But no matter what success she has, family will always be the most important thing to Ashanti.

Her mom and dad travel with her when she does shows. And she still calls Glen Cove home.

Ashanti also tries to stay down to earth.

"I think women should wear jeans and sneakers like the guys and still be accepted," she told Rebecca Louie of the *New York Daily News*.

Life has just begun for Ashanti. The young girl who once sang to Mary J. Blige now has her own songs to sing.

"It took me nine years to get where I am," she told *AOL News*. "I just want to inspire other people not to give up."

In 2003, Ashanti released her second album, Chapter II. It also went to number one on the Billboard 200 list.

CHRONOLOGY

1980 Born on October 13 in Glen Cove, New York
1983 Begins taking dance lessons
1989 Performs as dancer in Disney TV musical *Polly*
1993 Singing while doing household chores makes mother realize her talent
1995 Signs contract with Jive Records
1998 Signs contract with Epic Records and moves to Atlanta, Georgia
2001 Mario L. Baeza, chairman and founder of AJM Records, introduces Ashanti to multi-platinum producer Irv Gotti of Murder Inc.
2002 Irv Gotti signs Ashanti through AJM Records to Murder Inc./Def Jam; Releases first album, *Ashanti*; wins Soul Train's Aretha Franklin "Entertainer of the Year" Award
2003 Releases *Chapter II* and *Ashanti's Christmas*
2004 Releases *Concrete Rose*
2005 Appears in *Coach Carter*, her first movie role

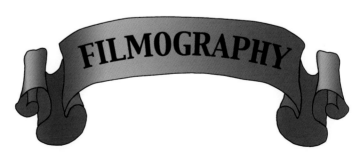

FILMOGRAPHY

2005 *Coach Carter*

DISCOGRAPHY

2002 *Ashanti*
2003 *Chapter II*
2003 *Ashanti's Christmas*
2004 *Concrete Rose*

FOR FURTHER READING

Books:
Ashanti. *Foolish/Unfoolish: Reflections on Love*. New York: Hyperion, 2002.
Bankston, John. *Ja Rule*. Newark, Delaware: Mitchell Lane Publishers, 2004.

On the Internet:
Ashanti Official Website
    http://www.ashantithisisme.com
Def Jam Records
    http://www.defjam.com/murderinc/ashanti
MTV News: *Ashanti's Fleet Feet Almost Kept Her From Becoming A Star*
    http://www.mtv.com/news/articles/1477735/20030829/story.jhtml

INDEX